GETTING TO KNOW THE WORLD'S GREATEST ARTISTS

BOTTICELLI

WRITTEN AND ILLUSTRATED BY MIKE VENEZIA

CONSULTANT SARA MOLLMAN UNDERHILL

CHILDRENS PRESS®

CHICAGO

For Tony and Becky

Cover: *Primavera*. c. 1482. Tempera on poplar on a gesso ground.
79 $^9/_{10}$ x 123 $^6/_{10}$ inches. Uffizi, Florence.
Bridgeman Art Library/SuperStock

Library of Congress Cataloging-in-Publication Data

Venezia, Mike.
    Botticelli / written & illustrated by Mike Venezia.
        p.   cm. — (Getting to know the world's greatest
artists)
    Summary: Examines the life and work of the Italian
painter of the early Renaissance, describing and giving
examples of his art.
    ISBN 0-516-02291-1
    1. Botticelli, Sandro, 1444 or 5-1510—Criticism and
interpretation—Juvenile literature. [1. Botticelli,
Sandro, 1444 or 5-1510.   2.   Artists.   3.   Painting,
Italian.   4.   Art appreciation.] I. Title. II. Series.
ND623.B7V37   1991
759.5—dc20   90-21645
[B]   CIP
[92]   AC

Detail of *Adoration of the Magi* on page 19

Sandro Botticelli was born in Florence, Italy, probably in 1444. His paintings were very popular and he became one of Florence's favorite artists.

Detail of *Siege of Florence*. By Giorgio Vasari and Giovanni Stradano, fresco.
Room of Clement VII, Palazzo Vecchio, Florence.
Scala/Art Resource, NY

Florence was becoming a great art
city when Botticelli was born. The
people who ran the city and ruled the
churches encouraged artists to create

paintings, and sculptures, and to
design new buildings. This period
became known as the early
Renaissance.

The San Barnaba Altarpiece. 1487. Tempera on wood,
105 $^5/_{10}$ x 110 $^2/_{10}$ inches. Uffizi, Florence. Scala/Art Resource, NY

The early Renaissance was a good
time to be an artist. Poets, writers,
sculptors, and painters were
respected and admired for the first
time in hundreds of years. Before this
period, very few people knew how to
read, and most people didn't care that
much about art.

Madonna of the Pomegranate.
1487. Tempera on wood panel,
56½ inches. Uffizi, Florence.
Bridgeman Art Library/SuperStock

Botticelli made lots of money by
painting beautiful works of art like
those shown above for churches and
the homes of wealthy people.

Botticelli's real name was Alessandro Filipepi. He became known as Botticelli when he went to live with his older brother, who was nicknamed "Botticello," which means "little barrel." Botticello was a gold pounder. He pounded gold onto

Detail of *Madonna and Child with Saint Anthony Abbot and Saint Sigismund.*
c. 1495. By Neroccio de' Landi, wood, 62⅜ x 55 ⅞ inches.
National Gallery of Art, Samuel H. Kress Collection

picture frames and onto certain areas
of artists' paintings, like the halos on
the people in the painting above.
Botticelli probably had the chance to
meet many artists and see their work
while he was growing up in his
brother's workshop.

Young Sandro Botticelli must have shown a great interest in becoming an artist himself. When he was 14 or 15 years old, Botticelli was sent to the workshop of one of Florence's

greatest master painters, Filippo
Lippi. In the 1400s, boys who showed
a talent for art learned about painting
and carving sculptures by assisting
master artists. It was probably fun,
but it was also hard work.

Madonna and Child.
By Filippo Lippi,
tempera on panel,
37⅖ x 24⅖ inches.
Uffizi, Florence. SuperStock

Botticelli learned how to mix
colors, clean brushes, and get walls
ready to paint on. He also learned to
draw and paint from Filippo Lippi.
Botticelli was greatly influenced by

Madonna of the Eucharist. 1470. Tempera on wood panel, 33 x 25⅝ inches. Isabella Stewart Gardner Museum. Bridgeman Art Library/SuperStock

his teacher. In Botticelli's first paintings, the colors, the expressions on people's faces, and the way he painted clothes look very much like Filippo Lippi's paintings.

Sandro Botticelli learned from other great artists in Florence, too. He worked as hard as he could to become better than the artists who taught him.

It wasn't long before Botticelli was asked to make paintings of his own. The painting on the next page was one of the first works that Botticelli was paid for. It was done for the wall of a meeting room used by a group of important men in Florence.

People who paid artists to do work for them were known as "patrons." One of the most famous and wealthiest patrons of Botticelli's time was the great Lorenzo de' Medici. Lorenzo loved Botticelli's paintings, and encouraged his friends and family to hire Botticelli to paint pictures for them.

Soon Botticelli had so much work to do that he had to hire other artists to help him. Botticelli's assistants helped finish his paintings, and even copied some of them.

Botticelli's paintings of Jesus and His mother were so popular that some sneaky artists copied and sold them without Botticelli's permission.

Today, it's very hard to tell which of these paintings were done by Botticelli and which are copies.

Botticelli made many religious paintings for churches in Florence and other cities in Italy. One of the most beautiful was the *Adoration of the Magi*. It shows the newborn baby Jesus and the people who came to visit him. One interesting thing about this painting is that Botticelli made most of the visitors members of the Medici family. Lorenzo de' Medici is shown* with his brother, father, grandfather and other relatives.

*Since the Medicis had a strong family resemblance to one another, experts can't seem to agree on which figure is really Lorenzo. Some think he's all the way on the left side, holding a sword. Others think he's closer to the center, with a blue robe and hat, while others think he's farther to the right in a black shirt with a red stripe down the sleeve.

Adoration of the Magi. 1475-78. Tempera on wood, 43 ^{7}/$_{10}$ x 52 ^{7}/$_{10}$ inches.
Uffizi, Florence. Nimatallah/Art Resource, New York

Botticelli may have included himself in this painting, too. Many people think he's the one in the yellowish robe all the way on the right side.

It was common in the 1400s for wealthy patrons to want their portraits included in religious paintings, but sometimes they got carried away.

Even though Botticelli was well known for his beautiful religious pictures, his most famous works were

Mars & Venus. 1483. Tempera on wood panel,
27 x 68 inches. National Gallery, London. SuperStock

paintings of mythological creatures and gods from ancient Greek and Roman stories. During the early Renaissance, people were very interested in the history of these ancient times.

The painting above shows Venus, the beautiful goddess of love, and Mars, the god of war. Mars is about to be awakened by some pesty little fauns.

The people in this painting represent the wonderful things that happen in springtime. Because so many people are said to fall in love during spring, Botticelli placed Venus, the goddess of love, right in the middle of the picture. Cupid is above her head. The lady in the pretty dress with flowers could be Springtime herself. The West Wind, flying through the air, is blowing warm breezes. The other people are the nymphs and gods that help make spring such a great time of the year.

Primavera. c. 1482. Tempera on poplar on a gesso ground, 79 9/10 x 123 6/10 inches. Uffizi, Florence. Bridgeman Art Library/SuperStock

The *Birth of Venus* shows
the goddess of love on a
seashell being blown to shore
by the winds.

The beautiful soft colors
Botticelli used, and the way
he made the people seem like
they're gently moving or
floating in air, have made
this Botticelli's most famous
painting.

During Botticelli's time,
some artists discovered things
that made paintings look
more real and lifelike
than ever before.

Birth of Venus. c. 1484-86. Tempera on canvas.
5 feet 6 inches x 9 feet 1 inch. Uffizi, Florence. SuperStock

25

Renaissance artists, like Leonardo da Vinci, Raphael, and Michelangelo, studied science, nature, and the human body in order to make their paintings and sculptures look as real as possible. They tried to show space and distance in their paintings, so that they would appear three-dimensional. This is known as perspective. The painting on the next page, by Raphael, is a good example of perspective and shows how an artist could make people look very real.

Encounter of Attila and Leo the Great. 1512-1514.
By Raphael, fresco. Stanza di Eliodoro, Vatican.
Scala/Art Resource, NY

27

Above: *Bardi Altarpiece*. 1484. By Botticelli, poplar panel, 72 8/10 x 70 8/10 inches. Gemaldegalerie, Staatliche Museen PreuBischer Kulturbesitz, Berlin

Left: *The Virgin of the Rocks*. By Leonardo da Vinci, oil on canvas, originally panel, 78 x 48½ inches. Louvre, Paris. Scala/Art Resource, NY

Compared with the work done by other artists of the time, Botticelli's backgrounds seem very flat, and his people look less realistic. Botticelli was more interested in making his paintings beautiful in a fantasy kind of way.

Detail of *Birth of Venus* on pages 24 and 25

Botticelli often used his paintbrush like a pen or pencil to outline, or add lines around, the people in his paintings. His line work helped give a feeling of movement to his paintings.

Botticelli lived to be about 65 years old. He is best known for his paintings, but he also made beautiful drawings and illustrations.

Allegory of Abundance. c. 1480s.
Pen, brown ink, and brown wash over
black chalk on pink-tinted paper,
heightened with white,
12 ^{4}/$_{10}$ x 9 ^{9}/$_{10}$ inches.
The British Museum, London,
Department of Prints and Drawings

Near the end of his life, it seemed like everyone started to pay more attention to the younger artists of the Renaissance.

Detail of *Inferno XVIII.* c. 1480-90.
Preliminary drawing in silverpoint on
parchment, completed in pen and ink
and colored in glue tempera,
12½ x 18½ inches.
Kupferstichkabinett, Staatliche Museen
PreuBischer Kulturbesitz, Berlin

For hundreds of years, Botticelli's paintings were almost forgotten. It wasn't until the late 1800s that people became interested in his work again.

Right: *Pallas and the Centaur.* c. 1482-83. Egg tempera on canvas. 81⅔ x 58⅛ inches. Louvre, Paris. Scala/Art Resource, NY

Above: Detail of *Mystical Nativity.* c. 1501. Tempera on canvas, 43 x 30 inches. National Gallery, London. SuperStock

Today, most people agree that Botticelli's decorative backgrounds, and the way he gave gentle movement to his people give his paintings a special beauty that few artists have ever been able to achieve.

31

It's fun to see real Botticelli paintings. Many of them have been cleaned up in the last few years. People are often surprised to see how bright some of Botticelli's colors are, now that years of dirt have been removed. The paintings in this book came from the museums listed below.

The British Museum, London
Isabella Stewart Gardner Museum, Boston, Massachusetts
Louvre, Paris
National Gallery, London
National Gallery of Art, Washington, D.C.
Palazzo Vecchio, Florence, Italy
Staatliche Museen PreuBischer Kulturbesitz, Berlin
Uffizi, Florence, Italy
Vatican